Series 117

This is a Ladybird Expert book, one of a series of titles for an adult readership. Written by some of the leading lights and outstanding communicators in their fields and published by one of the most trusted and well-loved names in books, the Ladybird Expert series provides clear, accessible and authoritative introductions, informed by expert opinion, to key subjects drawn from science, history and culture.

The Publisher would like to thank the following for the illustrative references for this book:
Page 45: Wikimedia Commons

Every effort has been made to ensure images are correctly attributed, however if any omission or error has been made please notify the Publisher for correction in future editions.

PENGUIN MICHAEL JOSEPH

UK | USA | Canada | Ireland | Australia
India | New Zealand | South Africa

Penguin Michael Joseph is part of the Penguin Random House group of companies
whose addresses can be found at global.penguinrandomhouse.com

First published 2023

001

Printed in Italy by L.E.G.O. S.p.A.

The authorized representative in the EEA is Penguin Random House Ireland,
Morrison Chambers, 32 Nassau Street, Dublin D02 YH68

A CIP catalogue record for this book is available from the British Library

ISBN: 978–0–718–18655–5

www.greenpenguin.co.uk

Penguin Random House is committed to a
sustainable future for our business, our readers
and our planet. This book is made from Forest
Stewardship Council® certified paper.

The Battle for Normandy, 1944

James Holland

with illustrations by
Keith Burns

Ladybird Books Ltd, London

At just sixteen minutes past midnight on Tuesday, 6 June 1944, the first Allied troops touched down on French soil when the first of three gliders landed beside a swing bridge on the Caen Canal, code-named 'Pegasus'. On board were twenty-eight men of D Company, the Oxfordshire and Buckinghamshire Light Infantry, part of the British 6th Airborne Division. Incredibly, the pilot, Jim Wallwork, had landed on precisely the right spot, despite it being nighttime and despite strong westerly winds. In fact, as the glider slid to a halt, the nose gently nudged the perimeter wire protecting a German gun position at the eastern end of the bridge.

Jumping clear of the wreckage, they charged the enemy positions, firing their automatic weapons and hurling grenades. The lead officer, Lieutenant Den Brotheridge, was fatally shot in the neck as he ran to the far side of the bridge, but apart from this tragic blow the airborne men quickly secured the bridge as planned, supported by two further loads of troops whose gliders similarly landed exactly where they were supposed to.

A few hundred yards to the east was a second bridge, code-named 'Horsa', spanning the River Orne, which ran parallel to the canal. Although only two of the three gliders allocated successfully landed there, the men swiftly and efficiently secured that bridge too. The initial D-Day objectives had been captured intact, as planned, and on schedule.

These troops were the first of some 20,000 airborne soldiers dropped in the early hours of D-Day. It was the task of the 6th Airborne Division to secure the eastern flanks of the invasion front and the job of two US airborne divisions, the 82nd and 101st, to hold key ground along the western flank, at the base of the Cotentin Peninsula.

The airborne landings might have signalled the start of the Allied invasion of Normandy, but the battle for France had, in many ways, begun a lot earlier. Britain and her allies in the United States and Canada, especially, had been able to amass vast numbers of men and quantities of war materiel in the United Kingdom – more than enough to win the day in Normandy – but the challenge was how to bring them swiftly and successfully across the English Channel into Nazi-occupied France. The Allies, despite gathering an enormous invasion fleet, still had only enough shipping to transport a fraction in one go.

The moment they landed, therefore, the race would be on to see who could bring decisive numbers of troops and supplies into the bridgehead – or battle zone – more quickly. Would it be the Allies, at the nearest point more than 80 miles away across the sea, or the Germans, travelling across land?

This was where air power came in. Allied air forces could slow up the Germans' ability to supply Normandy by destroying railway marshalling yards, locomotives and wagons, key bridges and roads and also the German radar and communications network. This often meant bombing and attacking at low level, which in turn meant ensuring there were no Messerschmitt or Focke-Wulf fighters hovering above as they did so.

Fortunately for the Allies, winning control of the skies was achieved after a long, bitter air battle over the winter of 1943/44, and by mid-April their air forces had secured air superiority over most of north-west Europe. This allowed the full weight of Allied bomber forces to hammer the enemy transportation network in the nine weeks before D-Day. And very successfully too.

An early plan for Operation OVERLORD, the code-name for the invasion, had been developed back in 1943, but it was not until British General Sir Bernard Montgomery was made overall Allied Land Commander that this was significantly enlarged.

Although the overall architect of the plan, Montgomery was answerable to his chief, US General Dwight D. Eisenhower, the Supreme Allied Commander, and was also working hand-in-hand with his navy and air force counterparts, Admiral Sir Bertram Ramsay and Air Marshal Sir Trafford Leigh-Mallory. Under him was a large tri-service and multinational planning team.

Rough plans were approved in February 1944 and presented on 7 April. The flanks would be secured with the help of airborne troops: the Americans in the west at the foot of the Cotentin Peninsula, and the British and Canadians in the east, between the River Orne and the Caen Canal and, 5 miles further to the east, the River Dives. There would then be five major landing beaches, code-named Utah, Omaha, Gold, Juno and Sword. Monty would have liked more troops in the initial waves, but shipping was the constraint. Although the invasion fleet would be almost 7,000 vessels, which included 4,127 landing craft of various shapes and sizes, that was enough to carry only 135,000 men plus accompanying equipment and materiel on D-Day itself. It sounded a lot but, as all the Allied commanders were keenly aware, it was not enough to guarantee victory by any stretch.

On 15 May, Eisenhower called a final commanders' conference and asked them all to express any misgivings they might have. No one voiced any. Everyone accepted it was the best possible plan for the resources they had available. The challenge would be to secure a foothold and then build up strength as quickly as possible before a major German counter-attack.

In the nine weeks before D-Day, Allied air forces dropped a staggering 197,000 tons of bombs on France alone; the Luftwaffe had managed just 18,000 tons on London during the entire nine-month Blitz. There had been huge concerns about civilian loss of life, but casualties, although still some 15,000 before D-Day, were a fraction of what had been feared. All bridges across the River Seine had been destroyed, hundreds of locomotives had been shot up and marshalling yards pummelled. By the beginning of June, 76 out of 92 radar stations along the Atlantic coast had been knocked out of action too. On 28 May, 78 Luftwaffe fighters were shot down – and the closest was some 500 miles from Normandy, demonstrating that most of the German air force had been pushed back deep into the Reich. Control of the skies of northern France, a prerequisite for any amphibious invasion, had been emphatically achieved.

By the beginning of June 1944, the invasion armada had been assembled and the troops involved consigned to camps all along the southern coast of England, with the British and Canadians in the east and Americans in the west. An immense deception operation, Operation FORTITUDE, had long been in action, with double agents and imaginary agents feeding bogus information and creating fake forces and even a completely fake army group spread across Britain. The aim was to keep the Germans guessing where and when the invasion would take place.

Meanwhile, final details of OVERLORD had been agreed and were being put into practice, with every man allocated the right aircraft, ship and landing craft, and follow-up forces and supplies ready and waiting too. The logistics were mind-bogglingly complex.

After the beautiful sunshine of late May, the weather in early June turned against the Allies. A delay of twenty-four hours was advised by the meteorological teams, but even on the night of 5/6 June as the invasion was launched it was not certain the predicted good-weather window would hold.

A massive further challenge was how to clear enough of the minefields laid by the Germans in the Channel. A particularly dense mine barrier lay 7–10 miles off the Normandy coast. Tides and currents, combined with the need for enough clear routes through for the shipping to support five invasion beaches, posed a massive headache for the naval planners. The solution was the biggest single mine-clearing operation of the entire war, as a staggering 255 minesweepers working in teams cleared and marked two channels running out from each landing beach. That it was achieved in rough seas at night ahead of the main invasion force is testament to the extraordinary skill of those involved. It remains a largely forgotten episode that deserves far greater recognition.

Meanwhile, airborne troops were dropped at the western and eastern ends of the invasion front. In the east, the key bridges across the River Orne and the Caen Canal were captured intact in a brilliantly executed operation by British glider troops, while, despite chaos, confusion and scattered troops, all five bridges over the River Dives were destroyed. German counter-attacks from the east would be blocked by the lack of bridges, while Allied reinforcements could use the intact bridges to support airborne troops and secure the all-important high ground in between.

In the west, American paratroopers were also scattered, but secured all their objectives successfully, even managing to kill the German general of the 91st Luftlande Division, which was holding the southern Cotentin Peninsula.

With airborne troops successfully securing the flanks, the main invasion forces neared the Normandy coast. Heavy bombers preceded them but, in their anxiety not to hit the landing craft, many of their bombs fell too far inland. Offshore naval bombardments were, however, very successful. The weight of Allied naval fire was immense. One shell fired from 6 miles out at sea by HMS *Ajax*, for example, hit the shield and breech of a large German coastal gun. Supporting the Americans at Omaha Beach were 183 heavy-calibre guns of over 90mm diameter and many more cannons. In contrast, the Germans had just 32 guns of 50–88mm diameter directly defending Omaha and nothing larger.

At certain points on Omaha, the Americans landing in the initial waves were slaughtered, but others got across the beach with comparative ease. German defences, hammered by offshore naval guns and running short of ammunition, were knocked out one by one. Fighting continued all day, but the outcome there had been secured by mid-morning. Proportionally, the Canadians at Juno were worst hit, but also managed to push the furthest inland. Utah Beach was captured with very few casualties, while the British suffered at Gold and Sword, but still managed to secure a clear toehold.

The German response was illogical and poorly executed. General Erich Marcks, the local corps commander, sent his mobile reserve – serviced by French trucks and bicycles – after the American airborne troops and then changed his mind. By the time they entered the battle on the afternoon of 6 June, it was too late: they were exhausted and were largely destroyed. Field Marshal Erwin Rommel, the overall German commander in Normandy, was away, his chief of staff was still drunk in the early hours after a particularly heavy dinner, while the precious panzer divisions were not allowed to move until Hitler gave the order.

Hitler was never an early riser and, even once up, prevaricated from his home in the Bavarian Alps. Not until after 4 p.m. on D-Day did he finally authorize the panzer divisions to move. The nearest, the superb Panzer-Lehr and 12th Waffen-SS Panzer Division 'Hitlerjugend', thus lost precious hours.

None the less, the Allies had still fallen some way short of their D-Day objectives, including the key city of Caen. The British advance from Sword had been held up by the best sited and equipped strongpoint along the entire invasion front, code-named Hillman. This had been captured late on 6 June and by the morning of the 7th the British and Canadians were advancing towards Caen once more. By the afternoon, one battalion of Canadian troops – around 800 men – and a handful of Sherman tanks were nearing Carpiquet, the airfield to the west of the city, when they were counter-attacked by the newly arrived vanguard of the 12th SS. Strong in both weaponry and highly motivated young troops, the 12th SS were a formidable force and had orders to throw the Allies back into the sea. Despite this, they managed to push the Canadians back only a couple of miles before Allied artillery and dogged Canadian defence stopped them in their tracks. In their frustration, they executed thirty-seven Canadian prisoners and some of the wounded were deliberately crushed by panzer tracks.

It was a highly significant battle that proved that, in the wide open farmland around Caen, going on the offensive would not be easy, whichever side was attacking. After all, the 12th SS had been unable to smash Canadian infantry and armour that had initially been badly undersupported. It also set the tone for the brutal and extremely violent fighting that would follow.

The Germans now began sending reinforcements as quickly as possible. There were numerous low-quality infantry divisions in Brittany and elsewhere, but it was on the ten available elite mobile divisions that German chances in Normandy depended. Fortunately for the Allies, because of Hitler's illogical decision to split up control of the panzer divisions and spread them far and wide, getting them to Normandy swiftly was not going to be an easy task.

Their difficulties were also greatly exacerbated by the work of Allied air power before the invasion, which had strangled rail movement across France. The 12th SS-Panzer Division had been the first to reach Normandy, followed by the Panzer-Lehr, arguably the best-trained panzer division in the German armed forces. They had been due to reach the front on 7 June and with 12th SS and 21st Panzer, already in Normandy, were to make a coordinated counter-attack that day. Instead, during the 60-mile journey from Le Mans, the Panzer-Lehr were harried all the way; now the cat was out of the bag, and the Allied air forces could concentrate on supporting the invasion directly.

The long summer days also helped the Allies and hindered the Germans: the moment the Germans ventured on to roads in daylight, fighter-bombers swept down upon them. 'Sitting along the road were burnt-out trucks and bombed field kitchens and gun tractors,' wrote Captain Alexander Hartdegen, 'some still smouldering, the dead lying beside them. This horrible scene was the backdrop to our journey.'

Not until the evening of 8 June did the Panzer-Lehr enter the line, but they were unable to attack until the following day. By then the chance of a swift coordinated counter-attack was slipping away.

The broken arrival of panzer divisions meant a gap soon developed between the Panzer-Lehr and the 12th SS, so the newly arrived British 7th Armoured Division, the Desert Rats of North Africa fame, were hastily ordered forward to try to burst through and then swing round south of Caen. Early on 13 June, the vanguard reached the small town of Villers-Bocage, 12 miles south-west of the city. Unfortunately for them, leading elements of a heavy German Tiger tank battalion had also arrived near the town overnight and caught the British by surprise. Although over two days of fighting the Germans suffered heavily too, it had been the last chance for the British swiftly to out-manoeuvre the enemy around Caen.

On the other hand, though the Germans were only able to move freely during the hours of darkness, Allied mastery of the skies allowed the Americans, British and Canadians to bring across a constant stream of supplies. While this meant ever more men, tanks, guns, ammunition and other materiel, another priority was building airfields. Incredibly, the first was open for business behind Omaha Beach on the evening of 7 June. By the 15th, five had been built, using bulldozers, graders and rolls of pierced-steel plating, or 'PSP'. By 20 June, a staggering twelve airfields had been built. As a result, fighter-bombers no longer had to fly back to England to refuel and re-arm, and ensured they spent more time when airborne over the battlefield and, in turn, more time shooting up anything German that moved. General Marcks was killed by Allied fighter planes, while General Leo Geyr von Schweppenburg's Panzer Group West headquarters was also badly hit and so too were the panzer divisions heading to the front. The Allies were winning the battle of the build-up.

Then a huge storm swept in. A key part of the Allied build-up was the creation of two Mulberry harbours, each the size of Dover. These astonishing feats of engineering involved constructing huge, 200-feet-long concrete blocks to create a harbour wall, plus a floating jetty. Each harbour was towed, in parts, across the Channel then sunk in place, but between 19 and 21 June the ferocious storm knocked Allied plans awry. The American Mulberry was largely destroyed and, although the British harbour at Arromanches survived, some 800 landing ships were also lost.

This meant that by the third week in June Montgomery was missing an entire corps of three divisions that he had counted on having in place by then. Aware from decoded German radio messages that more panzer divisions were en route to the Caen sector and that the enemy was planning a concentrated counter-attack, Monty and his Second Army commander, General Miles Dempsey, knew they needed to launch a major attack themselves in an effort to chew up new panzer units as they arrived and before they could organize themselves into a coordinated assault.

Before the invasion, Monty had predicted being 50 miles inland by the end of June, yet the advance had been nothing like as far as that, and with German V-1 flying bombs now falling on the British capital, impatience over the perceived lack of Allied progress was quickly growing in London and Washington.

On 25 June General Dempsey launched an attack towards the Rauray Ridge, key high ground some 12 miles west of Caen. British armour and infantry clashed with the Panzer-Lehr and 12th SS. In one action, a single Sherman tank of the Sherwood Rangers Yeomanry knocked out one Tiger, two formidable Panthers and two Panzer IVs.

The attack on the Rauray Ridge was to draw the enemy away from the main assault, Operation EPSOM, just to the west of Caen, which was launched the next day, 26 June. Bad weather ensured there was not the usual air support, while the rapidly increasing number of panzer units reaching the area, combined with a shortfall of Allied troops as a result of the storm and continued poor weather, made a decisive British breakthrough unlikely.

Attacking meant infantry and tanks advancing over open fields behind a barrage of artillery, which invariably never gave quite the protection hoped for by those advancing. Waiting for them were well-dug-in German troops with artillery, tanks, anti-tank guns, mortars and machine guns. Aware that Germans, without fail, always counter-attacked, British commanders were, in effect, using the infantry and armour as bait: the moment the Germans emerged from their foxholes and cover, down came the full force of Allied fire-power, from the immense weight of artillery but also from offshore naval guns and, when skies were clear, their air forces.

At the start of EPSOM, the British troops of VIII Corps pressed forward, making ground but 2 miles short of their first-day objective, the River Odon, which ran west–east across the axis of advance. German resistance was fierce and not until late on 27 June did British troops get across and start pushing up the far slopes towards a commanding rise known as Hill 112. The following day the high point was captured, but by then more and more panzer units were reaching the battle and being flung into the counter-attack. By 30 June, elements of no fewer than seven panzer divisions were desperately attacking the British salient, now dubbed the Scottish Corridor after the spearhead, the 15th Scottish Division.

The full weight of Allied fire-power now poured down on the German counter-attack, smashing these newly arrived units before they had had a chance to familiarize themselves with the ground or organize properly. Even so, fearing the British troops on Hill 112 were becoming isolated and in danger of being cut off, on 30 June General Dempsey ordered them to pull back to shorten the salient and ensure the front remained secure. EPSOM was halted and, while there had been no decisive British breakthrough, because the Germans had flung newly arriving panzer units straight into the fighting, their casualties had been so heavy that they had now lost their last chance of a fully coordinated large-scale counter-attack.

Meanwhile, in the western half of the battlefront, the Americans were simultaneously pushing south towards St-Lô and also north-west up the Cotentin Peninsula towards the port of Cherbourg. Here the ground was dominated by the *bocage*, a network of small fields fenced by dense hedgerows grown on raised banks. The bocage was every bit as difficult an area through which to fight as the wide-open farmland around Caen, but for different reasons. Here, it was hard to see what lay ahead, while tanks simply could not get over the raised banks and hedgerows. This left the infantry horribly exposed. Casualties among front-line units were appalling. The 4th Infantry Division, which had lost just a handful of men on D-Day, suffered 100 per cent front-line casualties within a fortnight as they battled up the Cotentin.

Rommel had urged Hitler to allow him to evacuate the Cotentin, but the Führer had refused. Instead, three entire German divisions were lost as Cherbourg finally fell on 27 June. Three days later, the last German troops in the peninsula were forced to surrender too.

For those back in London and Washington, looking at their maps, it still seemed as though the Allies were barely moving. On one level, this was true, but in this highly attritional phase of the battle the Allies were slowly but surely grinding down the Germans, chewing them up bit by bit and all the while growing in strength, while German troops and reinforcements continued to struggle to reach the front. In the same time that a million Allied troops reached Normandy, the increasingly battered German divisions received just over 10,000 replacements. Despite casualties, the US 4th Division was soon back at full strength, while equivalent German units continued to be flung into the fighting with ever-decreasing numbers of men.

Much has been made of the Germans' tactical flair and their ability to organize themselves swiftly into *Kampfgruppen* – battle groups. Discipline was certainly good, especially in the panzer divisions, but they also had less to organize than the Allies. With no Luftwaffe to speak of, fewer guns, vehicles and no naval support, they could coordinate actions more quickly. There was a freedom of manoeuvre because of their materiel poverty.

In contrast, the Allies had to organize and coordinate infantry, tanks, engineers and artillery, along with offshore naval guns and air forces. It was logistically tricky to plan operations across three services while ensuring there was also the strength in depth to support a major offensive. These were the constraints of Allied materiel wealth, and a lack of tactical chutzpah was the result. None the less, this materiel-heavy, steady grinding down of the enemy was incredibly effective. The lines on the map might have been moving slowly, but this mattered less than those in London and Washington feared.

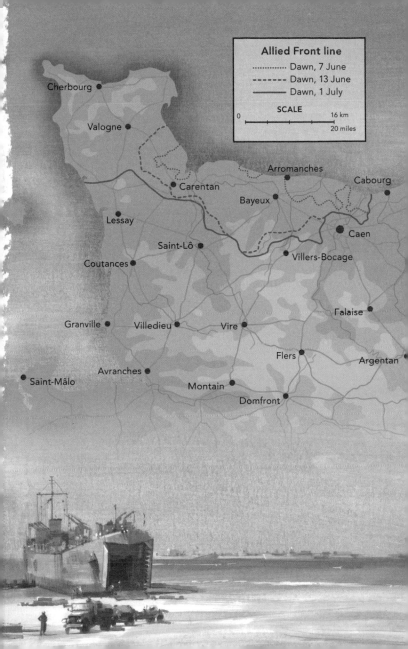

Allied Front line
- ········· Dawn, 7 June
- – – – – Dawn, 13 June
- ———— Dawn, 1 July

SCALE

0   16 km
         20 miles

Cherbourg

Valogne

Arromanches

Cabourg

Carentan

Bayeux

Lessay

Caen

Saint-Lô

Villers-Bocage

Coutances

Falaise

Granville

Villedieu

Vire

Flers

Argentan

Avranches

Saint-Mâlo

Montain

Domfront

One of the issues was Montgomery's prediction before D-Day that the Allies would be 50 miles inland seventeen days after the landings. That had proved false, but was based on previous experiences against the Germans in North Africa, Sicily and southern Italy, when they had retreated in stages. Quite reasonably, the Allies had expected the Germans to do the same now, not least because it made little military sense for them to remain within firing distance of Allied naval guns. Rommel had pleaded with Hitler to be allowed to retreat from Normandy, but Hitler insisted they hold firm and fight for every yard, and sacked General von Schweppenburg and Field Marshal Gerd von Rundstedt, the most senior German commander in the West.

The German commanders were exasperated by the Führer's interference – even those in the Waffen-SS. 'The constant use of piecemeal tactics enraged me,' wrote Kurt 'Panzer' Meyer, the commander of the 12th Waffen-SS Division. 'What had happened to the days of the big armoured offensives?' All they could do was fight ferociously and try to hold on for as long as possible. The brutal battle would continue.

None the less, they still held Caen and, after the British withdrawal, once more had Hill 112. This decision of General Dempsey's has often been criticized, but his salient was being attacked on both sides by elements of the 9th SS, 2nd SS, 10th SS, 1st SS and 2nd Panzer Divisions, and the risk of those troops at the front of the British thrust becoming isolated and surrounded had been too great. Now, though, with the front line secure and the enemy blunted, it was time for the British to swing back the battering ram and attack again.

With Cherbourg and the Cotentin Peninsula now in Allied hands, the Americans began pushing south on a broad front towards the town of St-Lô, but found it every bit as hard to make ground as the British and Canadians did around Caen. The Germans had flooded the low ground, making large areas impassable, while they tenaciously held on to the ridge line to the north of Caen. The dense network of small hedgerow-lined fields and winding sunken lanes was ideal for defence. The Americans had to prise each field from the enemy one by one. This would have been easier had Sherman tanks been able to burst through the bocage and blast enemy positions with their main gun and machine guns, and with the infantry operating first behind them and then mopping up. However, the tanks simply could not climb over the high mounds at the base of the hedgerows, which meant the infantry had to operate alone and were being decimated as a result.

On the ridge to the north-east of St-Lô repeated attacks by the Americans could not find a way through. An important and particularly troublesome feature was Hill 192, near the village of St-Georges-d'Elle, which had commanding views all the way back to the coast and which was covered by a patchwork of dense hedges and lanes. It had first been attacked on 11 June, but the Americans had failed to capture it. They had tried again, but by the beginning of July it was still in German hands and the men on both sides had dug in as artillery and mortar shells rained down and snipers picked off anyone who showed their head above the parapet.

A major assault on Caen, Operation CHARNWOOD, was launched on the night of 7 July when 467 heavy bombers flew over and pummelled the northern edge of the city in an effort to hammer German lanes and pave the way for the armour and infantry attack that would follow. Many bombs struck the city, which had already been badly hit, and made Allied progress through the town more difficult because of the rubble. Bitter fighting between the Canadians and the 12th SS also took place around the airfield. None the less, by 9 July British and Canadian troops had finally taken the city.

By this time, the 12th SS were so badly mauled after a month of fighting that they had been all but destroyed. 'They had gone to war weeks before with fresh, blooming faces,' noted their commander, Kurt Meyer, as he watched them pull out of Caen. 'At this point, camouflaged, muddy steel helmets cast shade on emaciated faces whose eyes had, all too often, looked into another world. The men presented a picture of deep human misery.'

Near St-Lô, the Panzer-Lehr had been moved to face the Americans and immediately launched an attack on 9 July on instructions from higher up the chain of command. Already under strength, and without any time to prepare, they hit a wall of American fire and suffered further terrible casualties. In one panzer battalion not a single junior officer remained. After this, the Panzer-Lehr went on to the defensive, its tanks being used as anti-tank guns and crews not daring to move by day. 'In general,' wrote Major Helmut Ritgen, 'we lived in the ground like foxes.' Still, though, the lines on the map seemed to be barely moving for the Allies. Impatience at the top was mounting.

While British troops were flung at Hill 112 once more, General Dempsey began planning a new major attack to clear the Bourgébus Ridge to the south-east of Caen and, he hoped, to shatter German resistance and finally break out of Normandy. At the same time, General Omar Bradley, the US First Army commander, was also making plans for a major attack from the north-west of St-Lô. Both Eisenhower and his deputy, Air Chief Marshal Sir Arthur Tedder, had high hopes for Operation GOODWOOD, as Dempsey's new assault was to be called, but Montgomery had more realistic expectations. He did not, however, share his doubts for a breakthrough with Eisenhower or Tedder because he wanted the full support of the heavy bombers before the attack was launched and suspected this might not be granted for a lesser operation.

Because infantry casualties in British Second Army had been high so far, Dempsey chose to attack with his three armoured divisions, a deviation from the prescribed tactics. GOODWOOD was launched on 18 July. The bombers caused huge damage, upturning not only Tiger and Panther tanks but even the newly arrived 76-ton King Tigers, and the British armour, following on, initially made headway. By the afternoon, however, progress was slowing. In the end, GOODWOOD achieved exactly what Montgomery had predicted: the British had advanced 7 miles and captured the Bourgébus Ridge, but there had been no decisive breakthrough. Some 493 tanks had suffered battle damage, but because of the incredible system of battlefield maintenance and the huge standardization of parts for Allied equipment, within twenty-four hours a staggering 218 were back in action and in forty-eight hours a further 62.

What's more, GOODWOOD had ensured seven of the ten German mobile divisions had remained rooted in the British and Canadian sector.

This was good news for the second major Allied offensive, Operation COBRA, soon to be launched by the Americans. That troublesome high point, Hill 192, was finally captured on 12 July and thereafter the Americans slowly but surely pushed the Germans back. St-Lô was taken at long last on 19 July.

Like Montgomery, Bradley also wanted to use heavy bombers to soften up the enemy before his attack, but together with the American air commanders chose a different approach. His bomber force would drop a massive 72,000 smaller 100-pound bombs over a clearly defined area 3.5 miles wide and 1.5 miles deep. These would pulverize any German troops without churning up the ground so badly that it would be impassable to the attackers who followed. A device for uprooting hedgerows – a giant fork that protruded low on the front of a Sherman tank – had also been trialled and some 60 per cent of First Army's tanks had been swiftly equipped with these 'rhinos'. A huge force of more than 2,000 tanks and tank destroyers was amassed, along with 1,000 artillery pieces. It was an immense concentration of force – more than for any other single operation in Normandy so far.

Bad weather scuppered the planned launch of COBRA on 24 July, but the next day the weather was better and, on cue, the bombers arrived and began blitzing the German positions. Smoke drifting back caused some to drop their bombs wide and on to the waiting American troops. More than 100 men were killed and nearly 500 wounded.

For the Germans, the bombing was horrific. Two-thirds of what was left of the Panzer-Lehr were destroyed and a German paratrooper regiment effectively annihilated.

Despite this, initially the American infantry struggled to make much headway. The armour was then thrown in with orders to carry the infantry and just keep driving forward. On 26 July, the dam finally burst as the Germans could hold out no longer. Suddenly the enemy was in full retreat, and in daylight too. New VHF radios had been put in the lead tank of each armoured column and in the fighter planes above so that those in the air and on the ground could communicate. This Armoured Column Cover quickly proved a great success, as aircraft were able to warn troops on the ground of German troop movements up ahead, as well as hitting targets and paving the way for an increasingly rapid advance.

Meanwhile, in the centre of the Allied line, Dempsey was launching his latest attack after the capture of Hill 112. With his units brought back up to strength after GOODWOOD, on 30 July he attacked southwards from Caumont with two thrusts, VIII Corps on the right and XXX Corps on the left. BLUECOAT, as the operation was named, was a great success, with VIII Corps, especially, showing a new level of tactical verve and flexibility and pushing the Germans back a further 15 miles. Once again, the enemy had desperately tried to stem the flow and so had sent yet more panzer and infantry divisions to meet the British assault.

At the same time, Allied fighter-bombers were attacking the retreating Germans following COBRA. Vast columns were smashed and left burning, while American armoured columns, hot on their tails, harried them. Near the village of St-Denis-le-Gast, a German column was trapped nose-to-tail for 3 miles. Some 100 tanks, 250 vehicles and horse-drawn wagons were left in flames.

It was now time for General George S. Patton's Third Army to enter the battle. His men had been building up in Normandy and were activated as Bradley took command of the new US 12th Army Group. With a key bridge that crossed into Brittany captured intact on 30 July, Patton ordered his men to press on south and west with all speed, while the American First Army, still flush with the success of COBRA, turned eastwards. These were frenetic days, the Allied breakout from the battle of attrition in full flow.

By 1 August, it was blindingly obvious to all the senior German commanders in Normandy that the battle was lost. Rommel had been badly wounded in an air attack back on 17 July, throwing the German command into further disarray. Field Marshal Günther von Kluge, now in overall command in the West, accepted he needed to pull his forces back and across the River Seine with all speed or face losing both Seventh Army and what remained of his panzer forces, now renamed the Fifth Panzer Army.

Hitler, however, refused to countenance such a move. On 20 July the Führer had narrowly avoided an assassination attempt and since then his paranoia had grown. He now mistrusted his generals even more and his insistence on micro-managing had worsened. Then came the bombshell. On 2 August, a directive arrived from Hitler ordering von Kluge to counter-attack towards Avranches on the south-western Normandy coast. An armoured force of nine panzer divisions was to be hastily assembled and, supported by a thousand fighter planes, was to strike west and split the Americans in two. It was to be called Operation LÜTTICH.

Meanwhile, Patton's forces were sweeping through Brittany, capturing much of the peninsula and effectively besieging the ports. Other units were pushing on south and eastwards in a wide thrust. With First Army still pressing east to the north and the British and Canadians preparing to make a further strike south from Caen, the Germans were suddenly in danger of being completely encircled.

Despite this rapidly worsening situation, Hitler still insisted on launching LÜTTICH. Von Kluge had assembled only four panzer divisions, not nine, and only one of them, the newly arrived 116th Panzer Division, was in good shape. However, its commander thought the plan was so bad he deliberately ensured they were not ready in time. Even worse, British cryptanalysts had decoded enemy radio traffic and so Bradley learned the day before that a German attack towards Avranches was being planned.

Throughout the Normandy battle, the moment German troops assaulted they tended to be absolutely hammered as the full weight of Allied fire-power rained down on them, and this was the case with LÜTTICH when it was finally launched in the early hours of 7 August. Although the town of Mortain was quickly overrun by the Germans, a key hill was not. Here a battalion of the US 30th Division clung on and could not be budged.

The German attack was soon running out of steam. The thousand Luftwaffe fighter planes were nowhere to be seen – a few hundred had attempted to take off from airfields near Paris but had been swiftly pounced upon by Allied fighters. Everywhere, the German advance was faltering under the weight of aggressive counter-attacks by the Americans and continued pummelling from the air.

One of the reasons LÜTTICH ended up being so half-hearted was that one German division after another had been turned north to face the advancing British and Canadians. The Canadians launched TOTALIZE on the night of 7 August, heading south from Caen directly towards the key town of Falaise. The plan was to strike south by night, wait for the heavy bombers to pound German positions, then advance again and wait for the bombers to come over a second time the following day.

As it happened, the advance south was so successful it might have been better to have cancelled the second wave of bombers but, such were the logistical complications of coordinating these operations, this was not possible. Instead, the Canadian and British ground troops were left twiddling their thumbs while they waited, allowing the beleaguered 12th SS time to organize some kind of defence. That afternoon Kurt Meyer threw his last tanks into the battle and they were, inevitably, hit hard. Michael Wittmann, one of the most celebrated and decorated panzer 'aces' in the Waffen-SS, was among those killed.

Meanwhile, the Allies were now preparing to launch a second amphibious invasion of France, this time in the south across the Mediterranean. There had been much debate over another such operation, not least because many of the forces involved had to be withdrawn from Italy at a moment when there had been an opportunity to exploit the success of the fall of Rome back on 4 June. The debate had continued, but the landings were eventually given the go-ahead in July, as it was felt the additional ports of southern France would help with the swift conquest of the whole country. In addition, General de Gaulle of the Free French was very keen to see French forces take part in the liberation.

Operation DRAGOON, the Allied invasion of southern France, took place on 15 August, with a mixed US and French force commanded by General Alexander Patch. Resistance was limited and the landings were a success, costing the Allies fewer than 500 casualties and opening up vital port facilities. German attempts at counter-attacking also floundered thanks to the sabotage efforts of the French Resistance crippling enemy lines of communication.

Back in Normandy, the net was closing in around the Germans as American forces from the south and west, and the British and Canadians from the north and centre – now bolstered by a Polish armoured division – pressed towards them. On 16 August, Falaise was captured and the remaining German troops were forced to flee down narrow country lanes before the neck of the so-called Falaise Pocket closed for good. In the valley of the River Dives, the crossing points became jammed with tanks, half-tracks, lorries and horse-drawn wagons desperately trying to escape the fighter-bombers and Allied artillery. Few succeeded. The scenes of carnage were appalling. One of the most beautiful parts of northern France had been turned into the Corridor of Death.

American, Canadian and Polish troops met on 19 August. In all, the Normandy battle had lasted seventy-seven days, so although the pre-invasion estimates had not been realized, overall the campaign was over thirteen days earlier than Montgomery had predicted. At its end, two entire German armies had been destroyed – only some 50,000 escaped, along with barely two dozen armoured fighting vehicles out of the 2,500 that had been sent to Normandy. It had been a brutal battle in which daily casualty rates had been, on average, worse than for the Somme, Verdun and Passchendaele in the First World War. Normandy was, though, by any reckoning, a stunning Allied victory.